Let's Eat!

Cooking with The Renaissance Redneck

by Lamar Richardson

Publishing assistance by BookCrafters, Parker, Colorado.
www.bookcrafters.net

Contents

Lamar, Carla, and Darby

Introduction

Everyone eats, and most people can learn to cook, even if only the basics. And then there are people like Lamar. People who eat and cook, and experience food on a whole different level. People who take the time to savor and celebrate every bite. And we're not even talking about feasts or fancy restaurants. We're talking about a plate of scrambled eggs. A perfectly made grilled cheese. A burger, hand-patted, seasoned and grilled, and in Lamar's case, dressed up with a heaping dollop of Duke's Mayonnaise.

To take this kind of pleasure in cooking and sharing a meal is to live in the moment. To be present and grateful. It's the generosity of spirit spilling onto the plate.

Lamar learned how to cook the way the best home cooks do: by being underfoot in the kitchen from the time he was a kid. He's a talker, so you can imagine him chatting away as his mom, the legendary Doris Richardson, moved from sink to stove, simmering vegetables pulled from her garden, dredging chicken in flour – fixing what she would call simple meals. But simple can be the most challenging. Ask anyone who's struggled to master fried chicken.

That little boy grew up knowing two things for certain: one, the minute he turned 18, he was never weeding another garden. And two, there's not one thing in this world that can't be improved by adding bacon. The way Lamar cooks it, giving it all the time it needs to be both crispy and chewy, the fat perfectly rendered – you could just about eat the plate its sitting on.

I've seen this man close his eyes with pleasure over a handful of peanut M&M's washed down with a splash of bourbon. Watched him sit by the water at a lobster pound in Maine, plastic bib strapped on tight, reverently dipping a chunk of claw meat into a cup of melted butter. (You don't have to ask Lamar how he feels about butter 'cause he'll tell you. It's the best stuff in the world and however much you're using, you'd be even happier with a little bit more.) But I've also seen him find something yummy about a piece of lukewarm pizza served up straight from the box at a staff meeting.

Food is one of life's great pleasures - and one that's always best shared. That's what this book is all about. Welcome to Lamar's kitchen, where there's plenty of bacon, butter, and bourbon and always room at the table for you.

Sheri Lynch
July 2025

Lamar in the kitchen

Foreword

I want to extend a huge thank you to all who took the time to send in a recipe. They were all wonderful, and I wish we could have used them all, but space was limited.

I grew up watching my Mama cook and was fascinated by the process. She was never in a hurry, especially with scrambled eggs. It seemed like she sat on that barstool forever, like she had all the time in the world. It was like her orchestra was the black cast iron skillet, and bacon grease, eggs, salt and pepper, were the instruments, and her old worn spatula was her baton. With slow fluid motions she brought the instruments together to create a breakfast, from which there were no leftovers. I personally made sure of that.

I'm sure I worried her to death begging to let me help her cook. When she made it my job to make the coleslaw, that was a really big deal to me. I was probably 9 or 10, I cut the head of cabbage into chunks, put it in the blender, added a capful of vinegar and a pinch of sugar. Blended it, put it in a bowl and mixed it with Duke's mayo, salt, and pepper. I became Mama's sous-chef and eventually moved up to the stove. I've loved it ever since. I'd give anything if my Mama could be here to see it.

This cookbook could have never come together without Carla, My Smokin' Hot Wife. She organized it, proofed it, and made sure it had some sort of order to it. She is my partner in everything I do. My Ride or Die.

The fact there is a cookbook with my name attached to it is due to the kindness of Sheri and Bob, who for some reason, continued to answer my calls many years ago and allowed me to say stupid things on the air. Without them, and the support of Max, Doc, Heather, Tony, and many others, you wouldn't be reading this. And speaking of "you," the listeners, I can't thank each one of you enough for your acceptance, support, and encouragement. Ya'll are for sure, the greatest listeners in the world, and that is coming straight from "The Corn-Cob."

*Prep work is important; two fingers of aged Scotch
is the perfect pre-cooking choice.*

Appetizers

Cheeseball

This is a party favorite! Our friends love it. This recipe originally came from Matt, a friend of my wife Carla's family from Alabama. He shared this recipe with the family, and it soon became a popular favorite. No other cheeseball could live up to it. It's different from your average cheeseball because it contains chicken. It's the perfect appetizer to share at a party, special gathering, or for the family.

When you bring this to your next event, trust me, somebody will ask you for the recipe!

Ingredients:
2 8 oz packs of cream cheese
2 packs of dry Hidden Valley Ranch salad dressing (not the DIPS)
2 4.5 oz cans of premium white chicken
1 2 oz bag of finely chopped pecans

Directions:

Mix cream cheese, dry salad dressing, and canned chicken until smooth.

Form into a ball and roll in finely chopped pecans to cover.

Place in the refrigerator to chill. Serve with crackers.

Enjoy!!

Cheeseball

Redneck Salad (formerly known as Seven Layer Salad)

Many years ago, I came across this recipe, and I fell in love with it. I now call it Redneck Salad because one of the few green things a true redneck will eat raw is iceberg lettuce. I know this because I am one!

My mama served salad a lot when I was growing up, and it was always the same: iceberg lettuce cut up, tomatoes, onions, radishes, and cucumbers, put it in a bowl, poured French Dressing on it, and set it on the table. If it was a special occasion or somebody important, she would sprinkle some Bac-Os imitation bacon bits. I had myself believing this was real bacon. Not only was it not bacon, but there wasn't a pig within a thousand miles of a jar of BacOs. Another example of ignorance being bliss. All we had to do was scoop it out and put it on the plate. Easy-peasy.

The first time I saw a salad bar, I was shocked, not by the variety of ingredients for a salad, but by the fact that I had to walk around and make it myself. After I got used to using salad bars, it became hard to find French Dressing. I finally settled for Thousand Island and still love it today. Another shake-up for me was adding mixed greens beside the iceberg. I could not imagine anyone eating that. Where I came from, any greens that dark, you washed and cooked them in a pot with ham hock and bacon. I know better now, but every once in a while…

Ingredients:

1 head of iceberg lettuce	Duke's Mayonnaise
1 bell pepper (any color)	2 medium tomatoes
1 purple onion	2 cups of shredded cheese (sharp or not)
8 slices of bacon	

Directions:

Layer 1: Iceberg lettuce, salt, and pepper to taste

Layer 2: Chopped bell pepper (Color of your choice)

Layer 3: Chopped purple onion

Layer 4: Duke's Mayonnaise (If Duke's is not available where you live, and you cannot relocate, do the best you can.)

Layer 5: Chopped tomatoes

Layer 6: Shredded cheese (I use sharp but you can decide)

Layer 7: Real Bacon Bits (That means cook fresh bacon and chop it up.)

Put it in the refrigerator for at least 30 minutes or until chilled.

You can use a 9-inch x 13-inch or an 8-inch square glass cooking dish, depending on how many you are feeding.

Redneck Salad—(Formerly known as Seven Layer Salad)

Ashley Palmer Fischer's Taco Bean Dip

Our listener, Ashley Palmer Fischer, submitted this recipe. Here's what she had to say about it: "This recipe is what my friends have asked me to bring to parties for the last 20 years."

Here's what I had to say after making this recipe myself: "This is a great appetizer. I tried it out on our small group, and we all broke into a rendition of *I'll Fly Away!*"

Ingredients:

1 9x9 baking dish	1 8 oz block Philadelphia Cream Cheese, full-fat
1 16 oz Bush's black beans	1/2 of a 1 oz packet McCormick Taco seasoning
1 15.5 oz jar Tostitos Chunky Medium Salsa	1/2 bunch green onions
1 cup nacho taco shredded cheese	1 bag Tostitos Scoops chips

Directions:

Preheat the oven to 400°F.

Layer 1: Using the flat back of the spoon, spread out the cream cheese on the bottom of the dish. It needs to be smooth and even, and it may take a while to do this.

Layer 2: Using a strainer, rinse and drain the black beans; put the beans in the mixing bowl. Mix in the taco seasoning with the beans until well combined. Pour the bean / seasoning mixture over the cream cheese in the dish. Smooth out the mixture layer with the spoon.

Layer 3: Pour one jar of salsa over the bean/seasoning mixture. Smooth out the salsa layer with the spoon.

Layer 4: Chop 1/2 a bunch of green onions, layer the green onions evenly over the salsa with your fingers.

Layer 5: Pour 1/2 a bag of nacho taco shredded cheese over the green onions, spreading evenly with fingers.

Cover with aluminum foil. Bake in the oven for 30 minutes or until cheese is bubbly in the center.

Ashley Palmer Fischer's Taco Bean Dip

Kevin Smith's Hotter Jalapeno Poppers

Our listener, Kevin Smith, must like bringing on the heat! The title tells you all you need to know! This recipe will definitely keep your guests coming back for more.

Ingredients:
1 lb of ground sausage
12 jalapenos
1 8 oz cream cheese, softened
1 cup grated fancy cheese (pepper jack, colby jack, or mozzarella)
1/4 cup grated cheddar cheese
1 tsp garlic powder (or to taste)
1 tbsp chili powder (or to taste)
1 tbsp cayenne pepper powder (or to taste)

Directions:
Preheat oven to 400°.

Slice the Jalapenos down the middle. DON'T scrape them out. The heat is in the seeds and pulp. If you scrape that out, all you have is a mini bell pepper.

Brown 1 lb of ground sausage, crumble and drain. Combine with other ingredients. Place a layer of aluminum foil on a baking sheet.

Spoon the mixture into/onto the sliced jalapenos. Bake for 20 minutes.

Kevin Smith's Hotter Jalapeno Poppers (photo courtesy of Kevin Smith)

Sides

Lamar and his brother Troy

Keith, aka Paw Paw
(See recipe page 18)

Collard Greens

Collard greens are my go-to side with any barbecue, pulled pork, ribs, or beef brisket. I love them so much I'll eat em for breakfast! Over the years, I've experimented with a lot of different ingredients. This is the recipe I have settled on.

The right sides make all the difference when it comes to barbecue. In my experience of eating barbecue at many, many places, I have discovered that really delicious sides can make up for mediocre BBQ. Bland, unappetizing sides can take away from a really good experience. Here is my version of the best collards you can eat!

Ingredients:

2 bunches fresh collards, about 2 lbs (you can use "bagged" but if you do, leave my name out of it).

1/2 lb. thick-cut bacon (for the record, I use Wrights, but that's just me).

1 large onion, diced

1 green bell pepper, diced

1 jalapeno pepper diced

4 to 8 cloves of garlic, diced (to taste — I love fresh garlic, so I use 8).

8 cups chicken broth

Red pepper flakes (to taste)

Hot sauce, Frank's or Cholula (to taste)

2 tbsp apple cider vinegar

2 tablespoons butter (I use Kerrygold Irish Butter, but I assume any real butter would work; just don't use fake butter).

Directions for the pot liquor:

Use a 6 or 7-quart Dutch oven or similar pot.

Chop the raw bacon into small pieces and fry it over medium-high heat. As the bacon starts to brown, add the onion, bell pepper, and jalapeno. DO NOT REMOVE THE BACON GREASE! It is the "nectar of the gods." Once the vegetables are soft, add the garlic. Add the garlic and cook for about a minute, then add the chicken broth, red pepper flakes, hot sauce, salt, pepper, vinegar, and butter. Bring to a boil and then reduce the heat and simmer.

I let this simmer for 2.5 to 3 hours before adding the greens. But if you don't have that much time, at the minimum, it must simmer for at least 90 minutes to be even close. Think about it this way, the greens are just the canvas for the flavors you paint with the pot liquor. I'm trying to paint the Mona Lisa, not a stick figure cat. It takes time for all of the flavors of the ingredients to come together. As the liquid cooks, I constantly taste it to see if it needs more salt, hot sauce, or perhaps vinegar. My taste and your taste are not the same. I like a good pop, but you might want it to be a little milder. Now, if you are the kind of person who doesn't love leftovers, this ain't for you. If I like something today, I'm still gonna like it tomorrow, and probably the next day. This pot liquor takes some work, so I put it in the fridge and use it to make more greens the next few days.

Directions for the greens:

As the pot liquor is simmering, remove the large stems that run down the center of the collard leaf. When you have removed all the thick stems, wash the greens thoroughly. Stack 6 to 8 leaves on top of one another, roll up, and slice into 1/2 to 1-inch-thick slices. Add them to the pot, cover, and cook for between 45 minutes and an hour, stirring occasionally. Start checking at the 45-minute mark, you don't want them mushy, so don't overcook.

Collard Greens

Pawpaw's Baked Beans

My father-in-law, Keith, better known to us and our kids as Pawpaw, was one of a kind. Loud, life of the party, could get away with saying the most inappropriate things, generous to a fault, and loved to cook. He loved his family and a good drink of brown liquor. I use his baked bean recipe and have never had any complaints, mostly because it's hard to complain with your mouth full!

I have made this from scratch, using dried beans soaked overnight and a variety of ingredients. I have also made it using canned baked beans. For the amount of time and trouble the scratch recipe takes compared to using canned baked beans, for me it's not worth the difference.

Ingredients:

1 28 oz can of Bush's Original Baked Beans
 with bacon and brown sugar
1 onion, finely chopped
1 red bell pepper, chopped
1 jalapeno pepper finely chopped
1 lb of ground beef 93% lean (for burgers, I always
 use 80/20, but 93% lean crumbles up better)

1 lb of ground spicy Italian sausage
1/2 lb of thick-cut bacon (you know I use Wrights, but your choice)
2 tbsp of mustard (yellow, brown, or Dijon, your choice)
2 tbsp of molasses (to taste)
1/2 cup of Barbecue Sauce (your favorite, I use Sweet Baby Rays)
Hot Sauce to taste

Directions:
Preheat oven to 350°.

Spray a 2 to 3-quart casserole dish with cooking spray. Set aside.

Set aside 3 strips of raw bacon for later. Chop the remaining bacon into small pieces and fry it in a pan over medium heat for 4-5 minutes, until crispy.

Transfer to a paper towel-lined plate. Put the onion, red bell pepper, and jalapeno in the pan with the bacon drippings. If necessary, you can add a small amount of olive oil to sauté the vegetables. Cook for 5-6 minutes until soft. Put these vegetables, along with the bacon, in a large pot.

Now, in the same pan, fry the ground beef and Italian sausage, then drain them and add them to the large pot along with the cans of beans. Stir all the ingredients over medium heat.

Taste before you add the mustard and molasses. Gradually add mustard and molasses to your taste. If you want some heat, you can add hot sauce. Once you're satisfied, transfer to the casserole dish. Cut the bacon you had set aside into 3-inch pieces and distribute evenly over the top of the beans. Bake uncovered for 1 hour or until bubbling and the top is caramelized.

Pawpaw's Baked Beans

Charlene Hu's Deviled Eggs with Goat Cheese

When I see "goat cheese," my first reaction is, "I'm out! No, thank you, I'm good. I don't care for any." To say I'm not a fan of goat cheese is a gross understatement, with emphasis on "gross". It is ironic that this is a recipe for "deviled" eggs, because I feel like goat cheese is "of the devil." If I'm being honest, the only thing I don't like about goat cheese is the sight, smell, texture, taste and name, outside of those things, I'm ok with it.

I do, however, LOVE deviled eggs and have never met one I didn't enjoy. As I reviewed the recipe Charlene Hu shared, I noticed that she uses Duke's Mayonnaise. Then, I saw that one of the other ingredients was bacon. I took these two things as a sign.
When you have Duke's Mayonnaise and bacon in a recipe, it's possible that not even goat cheese can mess it up. I felt like I must try the recipe. I did, and my streak of loving every deviled egg I've ever met is still intact! These were so good that I now know I can, from this moment on, eat and enjoy goat cheese, as long as it is smothered in Duke's Mayonnaise and wrapped in bacon.

Ingredients:
12 eggs
4 oz goat cheese
1/3 cup Duke's mayo
1 tbsp yellow mustard
salt and pepper to taste
3 strips of cooked bacon

Directions:
In cold water, place eggs in the pot and bring to a boil for 10 minutes. Cool and peel the eggs. Slice eggs in half and remove the hard yolks into a separate bowl.

Mash egg yolks and mix with goat cheese.

Then add the mayo and mustard.

Add salt and pepper to taste.

Place the mixture in a gallon plastic bag. Cut off a corner tip and then pipe into each egg half.

Cut the strips of bacon into 12 pieces and place a bacon strip into the yolk.

Charlene Hu's Deviled Eggs with Goat Cheese
(Photo courtesy of Charlene Hu)

Mama's Cornbread Dressing

This is an easy recipe; nothing fancy. You can add ingredients to it if you want. I'm big on experimenting with recipes, but this is all I knew growing up, and I wouldn't change it for the world. This reminds me of my mama in so many ways. She didn't buy breadcrumbs at the store; she let a loaf of bread sit out for a few days and get stale. Then she would make a couple of pones of cornbread and do it the same way. Then she would break it up and mix it. I've never tasted stuffing, I'm sure it's fine, but THIS is Thanksgiving for me. Never had it at any other time than Thanksgiving. So, I looked forward to it every year. She made a bunch of it, so I had it as leftovers for days, including breakfast.

Ingredients:
3 cups cornbread crumbs
2 1/4 cups dry breadcrumbs
1/2 cup chopped onion
3 eggs
32 oz chicken broth
1 stick butter
salt and pepper to taste
sage and/or poultry seasoning to taste

Directions:
Mix all ingredients.

Bake at 375 – 400 degrees until golden brown.

Start checking at 45 minutes.

For 5 or more people, you need to double it.

Lamar's Mom and Dad

Mama's Cornbread Dressing

Rick Keith's Mama's Chocolate Gravy

Rick Keith submitted this recipe along with this note: "This is one of my mama's (Bea Keith) favorite recipes. For years, my family and my brother's family met at Mom and Dad's house every Sunday morning for breakfast. Chocolate gravy was always on the table!! Since retiring, I have learned to make Chocolate Gravy, and when my kids come over for breakfast, of course, chocolate gravy is a must-have. The tradition lives on. ♥"

Where has this been all my life, Keith? And how did I not know about it? I have always been a gravy guy, but this chocolate gravy takes a buttered biscuit to a whole new level! God bless Bea Keith, and thank you, Rick, for sharing this!

Ingredients:
1 cup sugar
2 tbsp cocoa
2 tbsp (heaping) flour
dash of salt (1/8 tsp)
1 tbsp vanilla flavoring
1 1/2 cups milk
1 hunk of butter (about 3/4 stick)

Directions:
Mix the sugar, cocoa, and flour in a heavy saucepan with a whisk until no lumps remain.

Pour in milk, vanilla flavoring, and whisk until well combined.

Add butter and stir over medium heat until it thickens to a gravy consistency. Add additional milk if needed.

Serve over warm buttered biscuits.

.

Rick Keith's Mom's Chocolate Gravy

Carla's Vegetable Casserole

This is a family favorite! Carla's Aunt Flora passed this along to Carla's mom, and she passed it on to Carla. And of course, Carla has passed on to her daughter, Alex. It's wonderful to see great family recipes being passed down from generation to generation. That says a lot about how good it is.

Ingredients:
1 16 oz pack of frozen mixed vegetables
1 cup of mayonnaise
1 cup of shredded sharp cheddar cheese
1 cup of chopped onion
3/4 sleeve of saltine crackers

Directions:
Preheat oven to 375°.

Cook frozen vegetables as directed. While they are cooking, chop the onion and measure out the mayo and cheese. Drain the vegetables and return them to the pot. Add the mayonnaise, sharp cheddar cheese, and chopped onion to the vegetables and mix well. Pour the mixture into a 5 x 9 pan. Crumble crackers over the top of the casserole—place pats of butter generously over the top of the crackers. Bake in the oven at 375° for approximately 20 to 30 minutes, or until the crackers are lightly browned on top.

Enjoy!!

Note: Double the recipe when cooking for five or more.

Carla's vegetable casserole (photo courtesy of Carla Richardson)

Angie Honeycutt's Grits

"The first time I read this recipe, I thought, chicken broth and milk in grits? Who does that?!" Angie Hunnycut said of her submission. "Like any good southern girl, I had only eaten and prepared my grits with water, butter, and salt. But I thought, well, I guess I'll try this new way and see if it can stand up to the traditional recipe. I'm here to say that these grits are the creamiest and most flavorful grits I've ever had! I still occasionally make the traditional recipe, but these are next-level grits."

I agree with her on the standard grits recipe; that is the way I have eaten grits all my life. The only thing I've ever added to grits was some cheddar cheese. I felt like that was how they made 'em in New York–fancy like that. Then I realized, they don't even have grits in New York. Why mess with a good thing? But what if a good thing could be a GREAT thing?

I tried this recipe, and I'm pretty sure if New York ever came to its senses, this is exactly how they would eat grits.

Ingredients:

1 14 oz can low-sodium fat fat-free chicken broth

1 cup 2% milk

1/2 tsp salt

1 cup uncooked quick-cooking grits

3/4 cup (3 oz) shredded 2% reduced-fat sharp cheddar cheese

1/4 cup freshly grated Parmesan cheese

1/2 tsp hot sauce (Tabasco)

1/4 tsp ground white pepper

Directions:

Bring the first 3 ingredients and 1 1/3 cups water to a boil in a medium saucepan over medium-high heat; gradually whisk in grits. Reduce heat to low & simmer, stirring occasionally, 10 minutes or until thickened. Stir in cheddar cheese and the next 3 ingredients.

Garnish with a little extra shredded cheddar cheese and a few dashes of Tabasco.

Enjoy!

Angie Honeycutt's Grits (photo courtesy of Angie Honeycutt)

My Mama's Mayonnaise Biscuits

I was totally grown up and out of my mama's house before I really appreciated her biscuits. I grew up having homemade biscuits almost every day. It was either biscuits or homemade cornbread. During the week, if we were running late and didn't have time for eggs and bacon, she would make a pan of biscuits, and we would have butter and jelly or sorghum syrup. I thought it was a treat to go to somebody's house that had store-bought brown and serve rolls and "whomp" biscuits. When I had friends over, they went crazy over Mama's biscuits because they never got 'em at home.

One of my favorite meals was when Mama would make a pan of biscuits and put them on the table. Then she got out the mayonnaise, sliced onion, sliced tomato, and salt and pepper. That was for the meal, then we had butter, homemade jelly (blackberry, apple, and plum), and sorghum for dessert. We would split a biscuit in half, spread mayonnaise on both pieces, add a slice of tomato, a slice of onion, and sprinkle with salt and pepper, just like a sandwich. I can't even begin to tell you how good that is! Then, for dessert, put some butter on the plate, cover it with one of the jellies or the sorghum. Take your fork and whip it together, then sop it up with a biscuit.

Ingredients:

2 cups all-purpose flour

4 tsp baking powder

3/4 tsp salt

1/3 cup heaping Duke's Mayonnaise or other (at your own peril)

2/3 cup cold whole milk

2 tbsp of salted Kerrygold Butter (optional, but why wouldn't you?)

Directions:

Preheat the oven to 450°.

Line a large baking sheet with parchment paper or a silicone mat.

In a medium bowl, whisk together the flour, baking powder, and salt until well combined. Stir in the mayonnaise until the ingredients are well combined but not smooth; they should be just mixed. Put the bowl in the freezer for at least 15 minutes, up to overnight.

Add the cold milk to the flour mixture and stir with a fork until the mixture is well combined, but not smooth. Turn the dough onto a floured surface and roll it into a rectangle, a little less than an inch thick. Fold the top third of the dough towards the center, and then fold the bottom over that. Then roll out the dough to about 3/4 inch thick again. Repeat this process at least twice, more if desired.

You can use a biscuit cutter or a sharp knife to cut into 6 or 8 biscuits, depending on the size you want. Put them close together on the baking sheet.

Bake for 12 to 15 minutes, rotating the pan halfway through, until the biscuits are golden brown. Remove and brush with the melted butter.

Lamar's Mama's Biscuits

Mains

Young Lamar and Family

*Lamar and Looney. Looney loves Lamar's
Famous Grilled Cheese.
See the following page for the recipe*

My Famous Grilled Cheese

I got this recipe over 20 years ago when talking to a Panera Bread Manager. It involved their Tomato Basil bread, but you can use any "hearty" bread, Italian, sour dough, anything substantial. This is my brother-in-law Looney's favorite dish. He demands that I cook it at least once while we are on vacation in Florida every year. Trust me, it is not your normal grilled cheese. The biggest decision for you is what cheeses you want. Yes, I said cheeses, plural. There must be a minimum of 3, but I normally use 4. Some of the best cheeses for this recipe are Swiss, Mozzarella, Gouda, Sharp Cheddar, Monterey Jack, American, Monterey Jack, and Pepper Jack. There are certainly others, it's up to you. But it has to be real cheese, not that stuff that is wrapped in plastic and isn't actually cheese.

Ingredients:
Bread of your choice
3 or more cheeses of your choice (you can use sliced, but I prefer shredded because it melts easier)
Duke's Mayonnaise (or mayo of your choice, but I can't guarantee results)
Wright's thick cut bacon (if you choose another brand, results can and will vary).
Dry Italian seasoning
Kerry Gold Irish Butter (or any real butter)
Baking pan

Directions:
Put bacon in an aluminum foil lined pan. Place on the middle rack in a cold oven. Set oven to 400° and start checking it at 20 minutes.

Remove from the oven when the bacon is rendered and crisp. When the bacon has cooled, place it on a cutting board and chop it up. Reset the oven to 250°.

Spread mayonnaise on both slices of bread. If the cheese is shredded, mix them together in a bowl. Put about 1/4 cup of cheese on one slice of bread, followed by sprinkling chopped bacon on top of the cheese, then put another 1/4 cup of cheese on top of the bacon. If you use sliced cheese, put the bacon between the slices as you build the sandwich. Put the other slice of bread on top.

Butter the top of the bread and sprinkle with the dry Italian seasoning. Place buttered side down in a pan over medium heat. As that side is toasting, butter the other side and sprinkle with Italian seasoning. When both sides are golden brown, place them on a baking pan and place them in the oven at 250° so that the cheese is completely melted. When all sandwiches are done and cheese is melted, enjoy!!

Lamar's Famous Grilled Cheese

Smoking Hot Wife's Rahmschnitzel

Carla has made this dish for over 35 years. This recipe originally came from my wife's friend, Marion, who lives in Switzerland. They have been friends since their twenties. It has been a favorite with our kids and many of our friends and their kids. Carla gets lots of requests to make it. It is a little heavy calorie-wise but so, so delicious! You must give this one a try!

Ingredients:
Approximately 7 to 8 pcs - pork tenderloin pieces (thin cut – lean)
1 12 oz bag - extra wide egg noodles
1 1/2 pints - whipping cream
Butter
Salt
Pepper
Season All
Garlic powder

Directions:
Sprinkle salt, pepper, season all and garlic powder on both sides of each piece of tenderloin.

In a skillet, on low to medium heat, melt a few pats of butter, add the pork tenderloin and cook thoroughly, turning the meat to get a lightly brown sear on both sides. Add butter as needed to keep the meat moist. When cooked thoroughly, pour whipping cream over the pork tenderloin pieces and bring to a low boil. Then lower heat to simmer. Simmer for approximately 10 to 15 minutes.

While the pork tenderloin is cooking, boil the egg noodles until tender and drain them.

Place the noodles on the plate, then arrange the tenderloin pieces on top, and finally, pour the cream sauce over the noodles.

Ready to eat!

My Smokin' Hot Wife's Rahmschnitzel
(photo courtesy of Carla Richardson)

Tomato, Onion, and Mayonnaise Biscuit

Growing up, I had a lot of favorite meals. The fact is, I've probably never met a meal I couldn't get along with. One that really sticks in my head is one of the simplest meals my mama ever put on the table. It's one of the few meals that we ever had that did not contain meat. She would make a fresh pan of biscuits, peel and slice a fresh tomato out of the garden, yes, I said peel. Most people I've ever met do not peel tomatoes before they eat them. I still peel a tomato before I slice it. I will certainly eat an unpeeled tomato but if I'm slicing it, I'm going to peel it. Be careful, if you try it, you might not go back. She also had sliced onion and Duke's Mayonnaise.

Ingredients:
Mama's biscuits
Fresh tomato
Onion
Duke's Mayonnaise (or other if you want to take a chance)
Salt and pepper

Directions:
We would slice the biscuit open, put mayo on both slices, lay down a slice of tomato, an onion on top of that, and then hit it with a good amount of salt and pepper. Place the other half of the biscuit on top and enjoy! After a couple of these biscuits, you can cap the meal off with dessert of another biscuit with butter mixed with jelly, honey, or sorghum syrup.

Tomato Onion Mayonnaise Biscuit

My Favorite Version of Smash Burgers

Over the course of my life the one food that I have eaten more than any other is a hamburger. I can honestly say I have had at least 1 hamburger every week of my life. Of course, I have weeks when I don't eat one, but I also have weeks where I've eaten 3 or 4. I never get tired of hamburgers, the words, "I don't feel like a burger," have never come out of my mouth.

When I travel anywhere and spend a few days I look for a "hole in the wall" place that might have a great one. At a hotel, I will ask at the front desk or the concierge where the locals go for a burger. This has taken me to some really sketchy places! But, of all the places I've had a burger, the best one I have ever had is from a place in Spartanburg, SC, called Ike's. It's a definite "hole in the wall" with a bar, where you can watch them cook the burgers in front of you. There are a few tables for two around the wall, and a long communal table in the middle where everybody randomly sits and eats. They have a screened-in porch on the front and a fairly large deck on the back where you can eat outside. They also have the best boloney sandwich EVER. Three quarters of an inch thick, cooked extra well (burnt!), mayonnaise, mustard, chili, and onions!! It will change your life!!

Every time I go to Ike's, I promise myself, I'm getting the boloney. Then I go in, the server comes up and says, "What can I get you?," my mind says boloney, chili, mustard, mayo, and onion. But my mouth says, "bacon burger, mayonnaise, chili, extra onion, and coleslaw!" I find it impossible not to order the burger. Every once in a while, I will convince someone to go to lunch, on me, provided one of us orders the burger, the other the baloney, we slice them in half and swap. I get the best of both worlds!

When I cook burgers at home or when we are camping, I do it on my Blackstone Griddle. A few years ago, I started making smashburgers. You don't have to have a griddle; you can use a cast iron skillet, but you are limited to how many you can cook at one time.

This is my recipe, which includes grilled onions cooked into the burgers. If you don't want to use that part, you can skip it, and they will still be delicious.

Ingredients:

2 lbs ground beef 80/20 (less than 20% fat the patties won't hold together)
1 large white onion, sliced very thin on a Mandoline if possible
2 medium jalapenos sliced very thin (optional)
12 slices of American Cheese
8 slices of bacon, cooked and sliced in half

Buns
Salt and pepper
Garlic powder
Condiments of your choice

Directions:

Slice the onions and jalapenos (if used) on a Mandoline if you have one. If not, slice them as thinly as possible with a knife. Place the onion in a bowl and add salt, then toss it gently to distribute the salt evenly. Let them sit for at least 20 minutes.

Heat up the griddle and add some oil if needed. Heat to 425°, if you don't have a thermometer, sprinkle a few drops of water; they should bead up and evaporate.

Make eight 2.5-oz to 3-oz balls of ground beef, loosely packed (use a food scale if you have one). There will be two patties on each burger. Put a ball of hamburger on the grill and generously season it with salt, pepper, and powdered garlic.

Cover it with onion and jalapenos (if using). Cover with a piece of parchment paper, and using a burger press or heavy spatula press until flat. Remove the parchment paper and do this to the rest of the balls, making sure to leave 3 to 4 inches between the pre-smashed burgers. Cook until liquid starts to come up through the holes in the beef and the outer edges are no longer pink. The outer edges of the onion should also start to caramelize. This should take between 3 and 4 minutes. Using your metal spatula, preserve as much of the crust as possible. Flip and season. After 2 minutes, cover each patty with a slice of cheese. There will be two patties on each burger. Place two pieces of bacon on one of those patties, and then place the other patty on top of the bacon. Place 2 pieces of bacon on each patty.

Put your condiments and burgers on the buns and serve.

My Favorite Version of Smashburger

Kristin's Crockpot Angel Chicken

My wife, Carla, met Kristin a few years ago, and after getting to know each other over a few glasses of wine, it turns out they have so much in common, it's almost like they are sisters. Eventually, I met her husband Terry, and turns out, he's a great guy, and what do you know, he loves some brown liquor. That makes us almost brothers. They have 2 beautiful daughters, and over the years they have all become family. Kristin tried to act like she didn't cook, but it turns out she is a phenomenal cook, baker, and makes a mean cocktail.

Ingredients:
4 boneless, skinless chicken breasts
1/2 cup butter
1 packet Italian dressing mix
1 10.75 oz can condensed golden mushroom soup
1 cup chicken broth
8 oz cream cheese
1 lb angel hair pasta

Instructions:
Place chicken breasts in the bottom of the crockpot.

In a saucepan over medium heat, melt the butter. Add the Italian dressing mix, golden mushroom soup, chicken broth and cream cheese. Stir until the mixture is smooth and creamy.

Cover and cook on low for 4-5 hours or until the chicken is tender and fully cooked. Cook the angel hair pasta according to package instructions and drain.

Serve the chicken and sauce over the cooked angel hair pasta.

You can add more butter, a little more cream cheese and more broth to have some extra sauce for leftovers.

Kristin's Slow Cooker Angel Chicken (photo courtesy of Heather Furr)

Samantha and Gerald's Meatloaf

Samantha and Gerald are not just our neighbors across the street but happen to be great friends. They are always cooking up something and bringing it over for us to try and we do the same. Sometimes it's a meal, sometimes a dessert, and quite often (my favorite) a new cocktail! These are neighbors that we can count on to look after our house when we are out of town, and we can call at any given moment for a helping hand and of course that works both ways for sure. Carla and I are fortunate to have them as friends. And the fact that Gerald has never missed an episode of "Talking Lamar" ain't hurtin' a thing!!!

Ingredients:
2 lbs of ground beef
1 1/2 cups of cornbread crumbs
1 onion finely chopped
2 8 oz cans tomato sauce
1 egg
2 tsp mustard
2 tbsp brown sugar
2 tbsp vinegar
1/4 cup water
1 tbsp hot sauce
1 1/4 tsp salt
1/2 tsp pepper

Directions:
Heat oven to 350°.

Mix the hamburger meat, bread crumbs, egg, onion, and 1 8 oz can tomato sauce together. Add in the salt and pepper. Put the mixture in a casserole dish.

In a separate bowl, mix together the other tomato sauce, mustard, brown sugar, vinegar, water, and hot sauce. Pour over the top of the meatloaf mixture.

Bake in the oven for 90 minutes.

Samantha and Gerald's Meatloaf

Alex's Kielbasa and Cabbage Skillet

This has become one of my favorite things to cook because it is fairly simple and if you like cabbage, it's awesome. If you don't like cabbage, you will after you eat this. The apple did not fall far from the tree. My daughter, Alex is like her mom, she can cook, but because she married a man that loves to cook, like her mom, she likes to sit with a glass of wine and watch Eric, her husband, cook. This is a dish she does like to cook, and she shared it with me. I think what makes this dish really pop is the mustard vinaigrette that you add at the end.

Ingredients:

Mustard vinaigrette
1/4 cup olive oil
2 tbsp red wine vinegar
1 1/2 tbsp whole grain deli mustard
1/4 tsp garlic powder
1/4 tsp salt
Fresh cracked pepper to taste

Kielbasa and Cabbage
1 tbsp olive oil
14 oz kielbasa sausage
1 yellow onion
1/2 head cabbage
1/8 tsp salt and pepper (or to taste)

Directions:

Prepare the vinaigrette by adding the olive oil, vinegar, mustard, garlic powder, salt and cracked pepper to a small bowl or jar. Whisk in bowl or shake in jar to mix and set aside.

Slice the kielbasa in half-rounds, heat olive oil in a wide-bottom pot, add the sausage. Sauté over medium heat until browned.

While the sausage is browning, finely dice the onion. When the sausage is fully browned, add the onions and continue to sauté until the onions are soft and translucent.

While the onions are sautéing, chop the head of cabbage into strips 2 inches by 1/2 inch. Add the cabbage to the pot with salt and pepper. Continue to sauté until the cabbage is tender. Let the water evaporate as you continue to sauté the cabbage.

When the cabbage is tender, drizzle half of the mustard vinaigrette over the cabbage and sausage, stir to coat. Taste and add more if needed.

Serve warm.

Alex's Kielbasa Skillet

More

The reason this dish is called More is because the more of this you eat, the more you want. This is from years ago when my kids were small. They loved it. So, you might say this simple dish could be considered a kid's dish. But it is a guilty pleasure that I still love. It makes great leftovers for the next couple of days.

Ingredients:
2 lbs ground beef
1 onion chopped
1 can mushroom pieces drained
1 8.75 oz can of whole kernel corn
1 8.5 oz can of Lesueur English peas (don't say you hate English Peas until you have tried Lesueur peas, the only English pea worth eating)
1 8.25 oz can of sliced carrots
2 14.5 oz cans of diced tomatoes
1 16 oz cheddar cheese shredded
1 10 oz pkg of spaghetti noodles broken in half, cooked and drained

Directions:
Heat oven to 350°.

Add 2 oz of olive oil to a pan over medium high heat. As the onions start to soften, add the ground beef. After ground beef is browned, drain.

Add all other ingredients and mix together, then place in a large casserole dish. Bake for 45 minutes.

More

BLT With Peanut Butter (Instead of Mayonnaise)

This weird sounding recipe came from a Bob and Sheri listener that left a talk back, she did not leave a name, but she has changed my life forever. She explained that she grew up eating BLT's made with peanut butter and she never knew any different, until she was an adult. She could not believe people used mayonnaise instead of peanut butter. It's really hard to beat a well-made BLT with good thick bacon, a slice of ripe tomato, and fresh crisp lettuce, with perfectly toasted bread, both pieces painted with a layer of creamy, tangy Duke's Mayonnaise. But she made the exchange of peanut butter for the Duke's sound interesting, so I tried it. She was not wrong. I'm not going to say I choose the PB-BLT over the regular, but I do like the change of pace occasionally. This is the recipe for the perfect peanut butter, bacon, lettuce & tomato sandwich.

Ingredients:
4 slices of Wrights thick bacon
1 fresh beefsteak tomato, sliced
Fresh Romaine lettuce
2 slices of bread toasted (your choice, white, wheat, sour dough, etc…)
Jif creamy peanut butter (this is not negotiable, any other brand and you are on your own)
1 tbsp of Kerrygold Irish Butter room temperature
Salt and pepper to taste

Directions:

After cooking the Wrights bacon, the correct way, and you know the correct way if you are reading this book. Lay out all of the ingredients. Toast your bread. As soon as it's toasted spread the Kerrygold on the outside of each piece. Now spread a fairly thick layer of Jif peanut butter on both slices. On one slice, place the tomato, the bacon, and then the lettuce, salt and pepper and cover it with the other piece of bread.

BLT with Peanut Butter Instead of Mayonnaise

Medigan Quick and Easy Spaghetti Sauce

I work with a woman who would never stoop to using spaghetti sauce out of a jar. Sheri would say that I'm a "medigan!" And she would not be wrong. For an anniversary many years ago, I made a spaghetti dinner from scratch for my Smokin' Hot Wife Carla. I spent hours slicing, dicing, chopping, and stirring. It turned out really good, but I don't think it was worth all the labor for a regular weekly meal. So, I started looking for a way to have a spaghetti sauce that didn't taste like you dumped it out of a jar without spending hours making it. I found it. You are going to want the best store-bought tomato sauce that you can find to use as a base. In my opinion that is Rao's.

Ingredients:

1 jar Rao's Homemade Tomato Basil Pasta Sauce

1 lb 93% lean hamburger meat

1 14.5 oz petite diced tomatoes

1 small onion chopped

1 green bell pepper chopped

1 jalapeno pepper chopped

1 tbsp tomato paste

5 cloves of fresh garlic chopped

Red pepper flakes

1 tsp of Italian seasoning

Red wine

1 tbsp Kerry Gold Irish Butter

Olive oil

Salt and pepper

Directions:

In a pan over medium heat, pour in a couple of ounces of olive oil, let it get hot. Put onion, bell pepper and jalapeno pepper in the pan and sauté until soft. Add the garlic and stir around until fragrant, for about a minute. Add a splash of red wine to deglaze the pan to get all the caramelized bits and then put in your pot to use for the sauce.

Add the jar of Rao's sauce to the pot and turn it to medium low heat. Put the hamburger in the pan you sautéed the vegetables in, salt and pepper the meat liberally and brown it, stirring it into crumbles. If you find there is too much grease you can drain it.

Add the meat to the sauce, turning the heat to medium high. Add the diced tomatoes and the tomato paste. As it starts to bubble, add a splash of red wine, red pepper flakes to taste, Italian seasoning and the butter. If the sauce needs more liquid use chicken stock.

Reduce the heat to a low simmer for 45 minutes to an hour.

Sheri and Lamar in Sheri's kitchen (photo courtesy of Heather Furr)

Black Bean Chili

One of my favorite things to eat is chili. Years ago, I participated in a Chili Cook-Off representing Budweiser of Spartanburg. While preparing for this contest, I spent a few months making all kinds of different chili's and taking them to work so that co-workers could give me their opinions. After spending lots of time, money, and making more pots of chili than I care to count, I came up with what I like to think is the best one.

I like it with or without beans. If it's going to be beans, I prefer black beans. You can use kidney or any other kind of bean, it's up to you. This is my special recipe, which is fairly spicy, but you can control that with the hot sauce amount and either leave the serrano pepper out or put in a couple more.

Ingredients:

4 tbsp olive oil
1 yellow onion, chopped
1 green bell pepper, chopped
1 red bell pepper, chopped
1 yellow bell pepper, chopped
1 serrano chili pepper, chopped
2 jalapeno peppers, chopped
1 poblano pepper, chopped
8 garlic cloves, minced
2 1/2 pounds 93% lean ground beef
2 squares of dark chocolate (optional)
1 32 oz chicken or beef stock (I use chicken)
1 12 oz can or bottle of Budweiser beer
(Not Bud Light, or Ultra, and surely not
some crazy craft beer. The one and only
Budweiser Lager. Anything else and I can't be
responsible for the outcome).

1 28 oz can crushed tomatoes
1 14.5 oz can fire-roasted diced tomatoes
1 12 oz can tomato paste
2 tbsp chili powder
2 tbsp ground cumin
1 tbsp brown sugar
1 tbsp Cholula pepper sauce (or to taste)
2 1/2 tsp dried basil
1 1/2 tsp smoked paprika
1 tsp salt
1/2 tsp ground black pepper
2 16 oz cans black beans, rinsed
1 cup sour cream
3 tbsp chopped fresh cilantro
2 tsp coarse salt
1 1/2 tsp coarse black pepper
1 tsp of powdered garlic

Directions:

Heat oil in a large pot over medium heat; cook and stir onion, green, red, and yellow bell peppers, serrano pepper, jalapeno pepper, in the hot oil until softened. Add chopped garlic. Stir for one minute or until fragrant and set off heat.

Heat a large skillet over medium-high heat. Cook and stir beef in skillet, sprinkle with salt pepper and garlic powder. Stir beef until brown and crumbled, 5 to 7 minutes.

Pour Budweiser, aka The King of Beers, over the beef and continue to cook, scraping any browned bits from the bottom of the skillet, until liquid is hot, about 3 minutes.

Stir beef mixture into pepper mixture, add chicken (or beef) stock. Stir crushed tomatoes, diced tomatoes, tomato paste, into the beef mixture. Season with chili powder, cumin, brown sugar, hot sauce, basil, and paprika.

Bring to a boil and reduce heat to medium-low. Cover and simmer until meat and vegetables are very tender and flavors have developed in the chili, at least 90 minutes, stirring occasionally.

Mix drained black beans into chili, continue to simmer until beans are hot, about 30 more minutes.

I like to make this the day before it is to be eaten and refrigerate it. The flavors are even better the next day.

Serve with sour cream and cilantro. You might also want cheese, and crackers or cornbread. I say, "Just go crazy!"

Black Bean Chili

Eric's Hawaiian Chicken with Coconut Jasmine Rice

This recipe is one that my son-in-law, Eric, loves to cook, and I love to eat it! His wife, Alex, has taken after her mom, Carla, in that she can cook, but doesn't care to. Lucky for her, Eric, like me, loves to cook, and he is good at it. I always look forward to visiting them because I know he's going to make something good to eat. Coconut Jasmine rice can be used with other dishes besides Hawaiian Chicken.

Ingredients:
Hawaiian Chicken
2 tsp olive oil
1 lb boneless skinless chicken breast, cut into 1 inch pieces
Salt and pepper to taste
1 red bell pepper, diced
1 15 oz can pineapple chunks, juice, and fruit separated
1/3 cup chicken broth
1/4 cup soy sauce
2 tbsp light brown sugar
1 clove garlic minced
1 tsp ginger, grated
1/4 tsp red pepper flakes, optional
1 tbsp cornstarch
Sesame seeds for topping
Green onions for topping

Coconut Jasmine Rice
1 1/2 cups jasmine rice
1 clove garlic minced
3/4 tsp salt
1 13 1/2 oz can coconut milk
1 cup water

Directions:

Hawaiian Chicken

In a mixing bowl, add pineapple juice from the can (about 1 cup), 1/3 cup chicken broth, 1/4 cup soy sauce, 2 tbsp brown sugar, 1clove of garlic minced, and 1 tsp grated ginger. If you want it a bit spicy, add 1/4 tsp red pepper flakes. Mix together and set aside.

Preheat a large skillet over medium heat and add 2 tsp olive oil. Add 1 lb chicken breasts, cut into 1-inch pieces, and season them with salt and pepper. Sear it for about 8 minutes, stirring occasionally, until the chicken is almost cooked through. Add diced red bell pepper and cook for 2-3 minutes until softened.

Add the pineapple chunks and cook for an additional 3-4 minutes. Add the sauce mixture to the pan, stir everything, and let it simmer for about 5 minutes.

Mix 1 tablespoon of cornstarch with 2 tablespoons of water. Add the slurry gradually to the pan until the sauce reaches the desired consistency. Cook for a couple of more minutes. Sprinkle with sesame seeds and chopped green onions before serving.

Coconut Jasmine Rice

Add all ingredients to the sauce pot and give it a brief stir. Place a lid on the pot and bring to a boil over high heat. As soon as it reaches a full boil, turn the heat down to low and simmer for 15 minutes. Fluff the rice and set it aside until ready to serve.

Eric's Hawaiian Chicken with Coconut Jasmine Rice
(photo courtesy of Carla Richardson)

My Favorite Scrambled Eggs

I'm sure if you are a Bob & Sheri listener, you've heard me say many times, "There is a best way to make everything!" I'm not saying my way is the best way in everything I cook. That would be pompous and not true. What I am saying is, "It's the very best way I know until I discover a better way."

I've been cooking scrambled eggs since I sat on my mama's knee as she slowly stirred eggs in the cast iron skillet after cooking the bacon. At that point, those were the best scrambled eggs I had ever eaten, and I cooked them just like her for many years until I saw some other ways. Every time I saw something different on a cooking show or saw an article that said "Best Scrambled Egg Recipe" I tried it. Out of many different recipes, I took what I thought were the best ideas and created my own version of scrambled eggs. For the last 7 or 8 years, I've used this recipe. My Smokin' Hot Wife Carla suggested I add cilantro, and it took it to a whole new level. I have had quite a few people give me great, unsolicited accolades. So, until I eat something better, these are "my favorite."

Ingredients:
6 eggs
1 1/2 tablespoons of Kerry Gold Irish Butter
1/2 cup sharp cheddar cheese (or cheese of your choice, I also like a Mexican 3 cheese mix)
1/4 cup of finely chopped cilantro optional (not everyone loves cilantro, but if you do you will love this)
1 tbsp heavy cream
Kosher salt and coarse ground pepper to taste

Directions:
Slice the butter into pieces and place in a cold nonstick pan.

Crack the 6 eggs into the pan. Turn the heat on to med high. Stir continuously with a rubber spatula, don't whisk, making sure to scrape the bottom of the pan. After 30 seconds, take the pan off the heat. Keep stirring. After about 10 seconds, put the pan back on the heat. Repeat for about 3 minutes. (Adjust heat if they are cooking too fast.)

Off the heat, season the eggs lightly with salt & pepper. Stir in the heavy cream. Sprinkle the cilantro and cheese over the eggs. Stir the eggs until the cilantro and cheese are evenly distributed. Take them off the heat. If they are done to your satisfaction, plate them immediately, they will continue to cook in the pan, even off the heat.

Lamar's Favorite Scrambled Eggs

Jill's Vegan Dish – Vegetarian Mushroom Wellington

I'm pretty sure it is surprising to find Vegan food in a cookbook from a man who majors in bacon, butter, beef and all things wonderful. My son Clay's girlfriend is the most interesting Vegan in the world! One of those reasons is I actually knew her for months before finding out she was Vegan. She never mentioned it. Jill is the first Vegan I've ever met that didn't make sure I not only knew they were Vegan but explained the entire lifestyle in the first 3 seconds of being introduced.

She discovered the Vegan lifestyle while traveling through India, enjoyed it and stayed with it. She plays banjo, rides motorcycles, and enjoys all outdoor activities. She put herself through college, has a Graphic Design Degree, and I enjoy sippin' brown liquor with her every chance I get. I've had some of her vegan dishes and truly enjoyed them. Especially this one. Even without bacon and butter.

Ingredients:

1 pkg Vegan Puff Pastry sheets, defrosted
4 portobello mushrooms, stems and gills removed
1 cup sweet potato, peeled and diced
2 to 3 tbsp olive oil
1 bunch of fresh thyme (or 2 tsp dried thyme, divided)
8 oz button mushrooms, cleaned

1/2 cup walnuts
1 tsp fresh or dried rosemary leaves
1 large shallot, peeled and sliced
2 cloves garlic, minced
2 cups kale, stemmed and chopped
1-2 tbsp plain plant-based milk

Directions:

Preheat the oven to 375°, defrost the puff pastry according to package directions.

Place the portobello mushrooms, stem side up, and the diced sweet potato on a baking sheet. Drizzle with olive oil and season with salt, pepper, and the leaves from 2 sprigs of thyme (or about 1 tsp of dried thyme). Bake until vegetables are tender, about 15 minutes.

In a food processor, pulse the button mushrooms, walnuts, and 1 tbsp fresh thyme leaves, and rosemary until finely chopped.

Heat a tbsp of olive oil in a pan over medium-low. Sauté the shallot until translucent, about 5 minutes. Add the garlic and sauté for another minute. Add the mushroom and walnut mixture to the pan and cook down until softened, about 5-7 minutes.

Meanwhile, in another pan, sauté the kale with salt and pepper in a teaspoon of olive oil until wilted, about 5 minutes.

Bring the oven up to 425°.

To assemble the Wellington, open one puff pastry sheet onto a sheet of parchment paper. Roll with a rolling pin to approximately a 10 x 14 inch rectangle. Spread half of the mushroom mixture over one half of the pastry dough, length wise (approximately the same width as the portobellos). Leave a 2-inch border from the edge to seal the dough. Top the mushroom mixture with the kale, sweet potatoes, and portobello mushrooms. Add the remaining mushroom mixture over the top of the portobellos.

Use a pastry brush to brush the milk over the perimeter of dough. Stretch the empty half of the dough over the log of filling. Seal the dough at the long and short ends and tuck under. Brush the top of the Wellington dough with more milk and lightly score with a knife. Bake until very golden brown and crisp, for about 25 minutes.

Serve with gravy and/or cranberry sauce.

Vegetarian Mushroom Wellington (photo courtesy of Jill Canady)

Max's Oven Cooked Boston Butt

I not only have the privilege of working with Max every day, but I am also lucky enough to call him one of my absolute best friends. We met around 29 years ago when I started calling in to the show and we quickly became friends. We have had some great times over the years especially traveling with the show. He is a tremendous stage actor, has appeared in commercials, and done a ton of voice work. But his main job is making sure The Bob and Sheri show not only runs smoothly, but that it runs at all. When it comes to that he is a magician. Over the years he has been a great coach in showing me the mechanics of being on a microphone, and trust me when I say, it has not been easy for him, but he has shown a lot of patience and encouragement.

My recipe for smoking a pork butt is in this book, but not everybody has a smoker. Max is constantly cooking Boston Butt in the oven, and it comes out great, so we included it in the book.

Ingredients:

1 boneless pork shoulder (around 6 lbs)	2 tsp kosher salt
2 tbsp chopped garlic	1 tsp freshly ground black pepper
3 anchovies rinsed	1/4 cup olive oil
2 tbsp fresh rosemary chopped	2 tbsp coarse Dijon Mustard

Directions:

Preheat the oven to 450° and bring the pork to room temperature while oven heats.

In a food processor combine the garlic, anchovies, rosemary, salt and pepper. Add the olive oil and process until it forms a paste, scraping down the sides. Remove the blade and use a fork or spoon to stir in the mustard. Rub the paste all over the pork shoulder, loosely cover it with plastic wrap, and refrigerate from 2 to 24 hours.

Place the pork in a shallow roasting pan and roast, uncovered, for 30 minutes, until the top starts to brown a bit.

Turn the heat down to 250° and continue to cook, uncovered, for 6 to 8 hours until the middle of the roast registers 180° on an internal thermometer, and as you slide the thermometer in you can feel that the meat is very tender throughout. If juices are in the pan, (sometimes there are and sometimes not) pour off the juices from the pan into a heatproof container. Place this in the fridge, where the fat will rise to the top, while the meat rests.

When the meat is cooked, if you think that the outside of the roast could use a bit more crust/brownness, turn the heat back up to 450° and let it cook for another 15 to 20 minutes to give the outside a bit more of a crunchy texture.

Remove from the oven and let sit for about 20 minutes. Spoon the fat off the reserved juices in the fridge and pour the cooking juices into serving pitcher or bowl (warm it in the microwave). Slice the pork as thinly or thickly as you like, expect the meat to fall apart some. Sprinkle the sliced meat with a bit of salt before serving, and drizzle with pan juices if there are any.

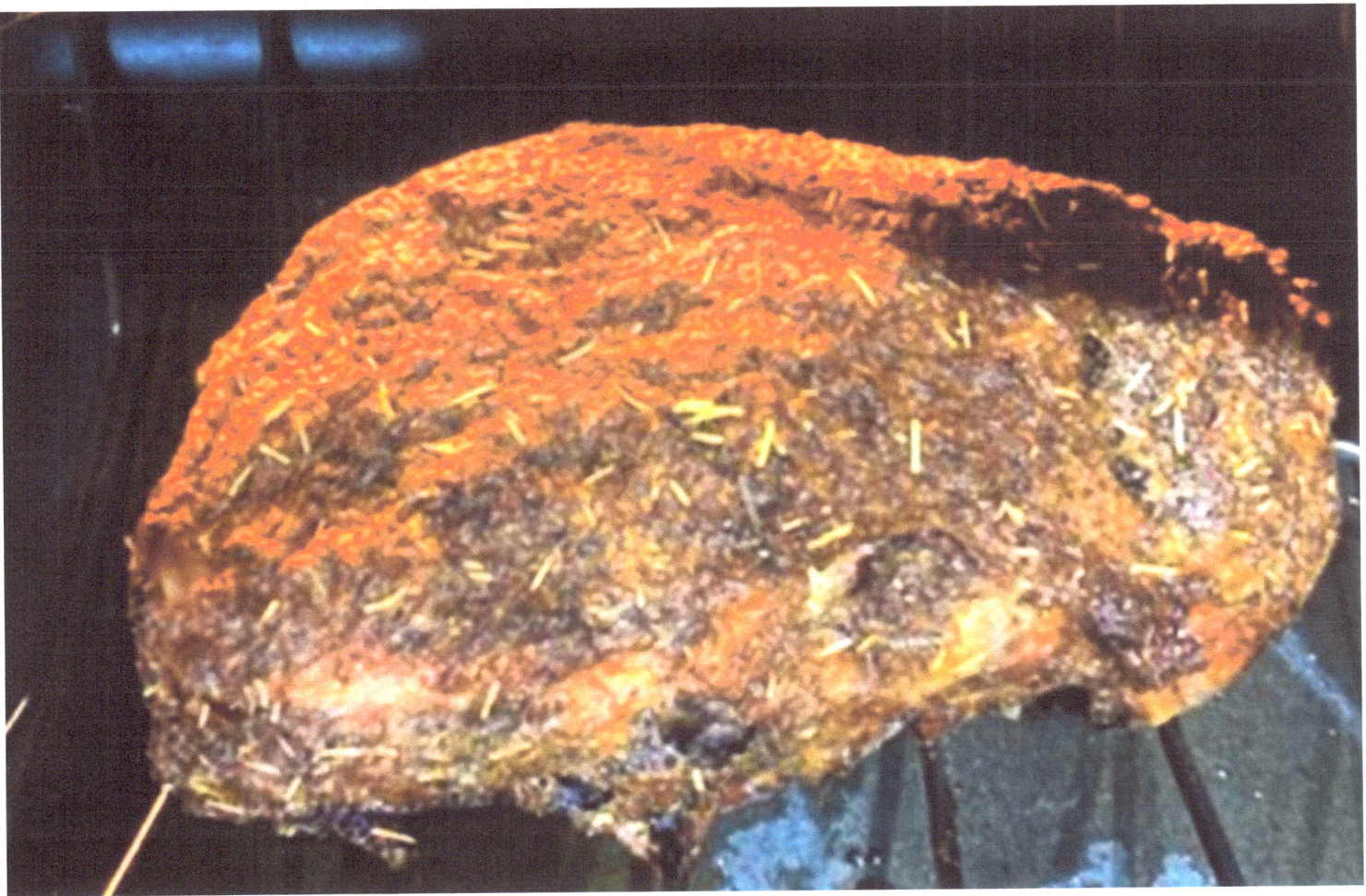

Max's Oven Cooked Boston Butt (photo courtesy of Max Sweeten)

My Recipe for Smokin' a Butt

Everyone knows I love food. When it comes to naming my most favorite food, there are two. The one I just got through eating, and the one I'm fixin' to eat. The one I cook the most is a Boston Butt. It's simple and can be eaten as a main dish with a few sides, or a sandwich. My favorite is on a bun with Duke's Mayonnaise, coleslaw, and touch of North Carolina hot vinegar sauce.

I cook my barbecue on a Treager pellet smoker. That is considered cheatin' by the cooks that use wood or charcoal and stay up all night. To that, I hold up both hands and say, "Guilty As Charged!" Those warriors have my respect, but if I can cook something and get the same result while I'm sleeping, count me in.

Ingredients:

1 Boston Butt bone-in (The bone makes it easier to handle.)

Olive oil

Yellow mustard

Kosher salt

Coarse black pepper

Garlic powder

Rubber gloves (multiple pairs)

Dry rub of your choice (I use Butt Rub but it's your choice)

Directions:

Pre-heat your smoker and get it to 225°.

I put down a few sheets of pink butcher paper under my cutting board so that I don't leave a mess. Unwrap the butt and dry it with paper towels. Lay the butt fat cap up, you will see why later. Put on rubber gloves and pour some olive oil on the butt and rub all over where you can reach without turning it over. Do the same with the yellow mustard. This is your binder for the seasoning.

Salt it first, generously, then the black pepper, also generously, and then the garlic powder, even more generously than the first two. Make sure you get it on all sides so that the entire surface of the butt is covered. Now flip the butt over so that the fat cap is on the bottom. Repeat the same process on the top of the butt.

Some people say "Fat Cap up so the fat will run down and keep the butt moist" (this is the only context where that word should be used). That is not true. The butt is dead tissue that cannot absorb fat running over it. If you put the fat cap on the bottom it does two things. First, it protects the bottom of the butt from the heat and keeps it from drying out, but the second reason is even better and tastier. At the end of the cook, that fat has rendered into the most delicious, what I call "bacon candy," that you can enjoy as a bonus for your hard work.

You can put a tray of water, or beer, or a mixture of all three in the cooker to keep it moist. Once you have the butt on the smoker leave it alone. The temp you are looking for is 205° for it to be done. If you have a way to monitor the temp constantly that is great, but if you have an 8lb to 10lb butt you are looking at 12 hours or more. When the butt hits between 155°and 165° it will go into "the stall". It will stay there for 6 or 7 hours. You have two choices, wait it out, or take it off and wrap it in foil and put it back on to accelerate the cooking time. There are pluses and minuses in both. I do not EVER wrap my butt, well, at least not my pork butt. Wrapping it in foil interferes with the "bark," that crusty outside that is so very delicious and is the mark of a great smoked butt. But that's just me, over time I encourage you to try it both ways and decide what you like.

Once you can put a thermometer dead in the middle of the butt and it is 205° pull it off, and now you can wrap it. The bark will not be hurt. Get a small ice chest and put folded towels in the bottom, place the wrapped butt on the towels and cover it with more towels and shut the cooler. Leave it for at the very least 1 hour. The meat needs to rest so that the moisture can re-distribute evenly through the meat. If it doesn't rest, you will have dry barbecue. To tell you how important resting is, I have a small Yeti and I leave a butt in there to rest for up to 4 hours before I pull it. You have to be careful that the butt does not cool below 145° to be safe. 1 hour is the minimum. Unwrap and get two forks and start shredding and pulling! Enjoy!

Lamar's Smoked Pork Butt

Desserts

Janice—Greatest Mother-in-Law ever—
See Nana's Coconut Cake recipe on the next page

Nana's Coconut Cake (greatest mother-in-law ever)

Coconut cake is one of my top three cakes and a really good one is very hard to find. My mother-in-law Janice, better known as Nana with our kids, God rest her soul, had it dialed in. It tasted great and was so moist (this is the only place this word should ever be used). It needs to be refrigerated. It is the best coconut cake I've ever had. Janice was my second mom and I really miss her.

Cake Ingredients:

1 box yellow cake mix

1 cup water

4 egg yolks

1 egg white

1 pkg vanilla instant pudding

1/2 cup Crisco oil

Filling Ingredients:

1 1/2 cup of sugar

1/2 cup water

1 8 oz pkg sour cream

1 24 oz frozen coconut

Directions:

Preheat oven to 325°.

Combine the cake mix and pudding mix and sift twice.

Then combine the sifted cake and pudding mix, eggs, oil, water and mix well. Divide the batter equally into 4 cake pans and bake at 325 degrees for approx. 15 minutes or until done. Cool. Combine filling ingredients and mix. Spread between layers and on the outer layer of the cake.

Refrigerate. Ready to serve!

Nana's Coconut Cake (photo courtesy of Carla Richardson)

Randy Cotton's Mother's Banana Pudding Recipe

Randy says, "Banana Pudding is a southern dessert staple that finds itself alongside the likes of the most cherished fried chicken church dinners with ham biscuits and potato salad. Discover a pork barbecue restaurant in the southern United States and you can bet banana pudding will likely be on the menu. Banana pudding is time honored; often crafted by the wrinkled hands of someone's loving mother and count yourself fortunate if she taught you how to make this wonderful, easy dessert. Such was my case with this recipe. It's a tribute to her every time it graces my table."

Like Randy, I grew up with banana pudding being a regular fixture on our dinner table. It was no less common than sweet tea, handmade biscuits, and canned pears with a dollop of Duke's Mayonnaise, sprinkled with shredded cheddar cheese. Each banana pudding, no matter the mother or grandmother that made them, was off the chain good! Each a little different with their own special touch, but all great!

Ingredients:
2 eggs, beaten
1 1/2 cups sugar
1 12-oz can evaporated milk
12 oz. water
1/2 cup sifted self-rising flour
1 tsp vanilla
3 bananas cut up in circles
1 box of vanilla wafers

Directions:
Combine eggs, sugar, evaporated milk, water, flour, and vanilla.

Cook this mixture over medium heat in a double boiler, stirring constantly until thickened.

In a deep dish, pour 1/2 of mixture over a layer of vanilla wafers and a layer of bananas. Make another layer of wafer and bananas and pour the remaining mixture (pudding) over that. You will use about 3/4 of the box of wafers. Make sure to press any bananas and wafers into the pudding that are on top. Let the completed pudding cool for a while before digging in. Refrigerate leftovers.

Randy Cotton's Mother's Banana Pudding
(photo courtesy of Randy Cotton)

Tony Tindol's No Peek Pound Cake

Tony's Granny Mae made this cake for Tony when he was a little boy. The secret is the temperature and NOT to peek in the oven while it's cooking.

My Wife Carla and I were able to hang out with Tony and Kyle at Margaritaville at Fort Myers Beach, FL. They are long-time listeners and drove quite a few miles to see us while we were there with some winners of a contest in which we recognized excellent teachers. We shared a few cocktails and some great conversation and a lot of laughs. We had a great time hanging out at the pool in their luxurious cabana!

"Them boys know how to travel!"

Ingredients:
1 stick butter, softened
3 cups sugar
5 eggs
3 cups cake flour (Wondra Brand)
1 cup whole milk
2 tsp good vanilla extract
Bundt pan greased and floured

Directions:
In a large bowl, cream together the butter and sugar using a mixer until smooth. Add the eggs one at a time, making sure to beat well after each addition. Gradually add the flour and milk, alternating between the two, starting and ending with the flour. Stir in the vanilla extract.

Pour the batter into the prepared greased and floured Bundt pan.

Place the pan in a COLD oven, then set the oven to 325°. Bake for 1 hour. After that, increase the temperature to 350° and bake for an additional 30 minutes.

Do NOT open the oven door while the cake is baking. No peeking!

Once done, let the cake cool in the pan for 10 minutes before turning it out onto a wire rack to cool completely.

Tony Tindal's No Peek Pound Cake (photo courtesy of Tony Tindal)

White Wine Cake

Allen O'Shields is a good friend of mine and was a co-worker at Budweiser of Spartanburg for 37 years. His wonderful wife Sally cooked this cake for our rehearsal dinner when I married my "Smokin' Hot Wife" Carla. Sally shared the recipe with me, and it has become the go-to dessert recipe for me. I have made this cake well over 30 times over the years. It's not without its dangers because it's not overly sweet, it's very hard to stop eating it.- Lamar

Ingredients:

Cake:

Bundt pan
1 box Duncan Hines Deluxe II yellow cake mix
1 3-oz box instant vanilla pudding mix
3/4 cup water
3/4 cup vegetable oil
1/4 cup white wine
4 eggs
1/4 cup sugar
2 tsp cinnamon
1/2 cup chopped pecans

Glaze:

1 stick butter
1 cup sugar
1/4 cup water
1/4 cup white wine

Directions:

Cake:

Heat oven to 325°.

Grease bundt pan. Put chopped pecans in the bottom of bundt pan. Mix all other ingredients together and pour it in the pan. Bake for 1 hour. 10 minutes before cake is done, make glaze.

Glaze:

Bring butter, sugar, and water to boil. Boil for two to three minutes. Remove from heat and add wine. When the cake comes from the oven, pour half of the glaze over the cake immediately. After 10 minutes, turn the cake out onto plate and pour the remaining glaze over the cake.

White Wine Cake

Japanese Fruit Pie

Let me say up front, Carla is okay with me putting this in here! She loves it too!

This is my first wife, Rhonda's recipe, and is a treat that we only have at Thanksgiving and Christmas. Carla and I share the holidays with Rhonda and her husband Bill so that we can all be with our kids. This is one of our favorites.

This pie is too dangerous to be a year-round dessert. I didn't know why it was called Japanese Fruit Pie, turns out it's because many years ago Southerners once thought coconut came from Japan. They also called tropical fruitcakes "Japanese fruitcakes." It's similar to a chess pie and pecan pie, and includes coconut, raisins and pecans. It has a light, brown crust and a crunchy texture. It's so rich it'll make your teeth hurt but you can't quit eatin' it!

Ingredients:
1 9-inch unbaked pie shell
2 eggs (beaten)
1/2 cup raisins
1/2 cup chopped pecans
1/2 cup shredded coconut
1 cup sugar
1 stick melted butter

Directions:
Preheat oven to 300°.

In medium mixing bowl, combine eggs, butter and sugar. Beat until smooth.

Stir in pecans, coconut and raisins.

Pour mixture into pastry shell.

Bake 50-60 minutes. It should be golden brown on top.

Japanese Fruit Pie

Carla's Cheesecake Pie

This is a simple pie that's so easy to make which makes it a quick and easy dessert for those times you need something homemade but not much time to do it. This is it!! You may want to make two of them because once you try a piece, you're gonna want to keep one for yourself. Plus, your kids and grandkids will love it. A must try!!

Ingredients:

1 8 oz cream cheese
1 can of Eagle Brand Milk
1/4 cup of fresh lemon juice
1 tsp of vanilla flavoring
1 graham cracker crust

Directions:

Mix cream cheese and Eagle Brand Milk until smooth. Add lemon juice gradually and mix. Once it's smooth, add vanilla flavoring and mix. Pour into the graham cracker crust.

Refrigerate for 4 hours before serving.

Enjoy!!

Cheesecake Pie (photo courtesy of Carla Richardson)

Abby Kimball's International Award-Winning Elvis' Peanut Butter Banana and Bacon Scone

I had the pleasure of sampling this delicious, sweet, yet savory dish at the Scone Goddess Festival in Northport, Maine where it captured first place among some tough competition. The combination of the salty bacon, combined with the peanut butter's velvet like deliciousness, that is gently kissed by the exotic creamy tropical tang of the banana, makes this scone a "Hunka-Hunka Burning Love!" "I just "Can't Help Falling in Love" with this dessert that leaves me "All Shook Up." Yes, I fully realize those are horrible puns, but "What I'd Say" is "That's All Right" just "Don't be Cruel" and "Love Me Tender!" OK, I promise I'm done.

Ingredients:
Scones:

2 medium bananas, either thawed and strained or overripe, mashed
1/3 cup heavy cream
1 large egg
1 tsp vanilla or vanilla paste
2 cups all-purpose flour

1/3 cup light brown sugar
2-1/2 tsp baking powder
1/2 tsp salt
1/2 cup (1 stick) cold butter (salted or unsalted), cut into small pieces
2/3 cup peanut butter chips

Peanut butter glaze:

4 tbsp milk
2/3 cup powdered sugar
2 tbsp smooth peanut butter
1/4 tsp vanilla or vanilla paste
Pinch of salt
The glaze should have a drizzle consistency. If it seems to thin, add more powdered sugar. If it's too thick, add a splash more milk.

Topping:

4-6 slices bacon, cook until crispy, cool and chop or crumble.

Directions:

Preheat oven to 400 degrees.

In a stand mixer or in a large bowl with a hand mixer, combine banana, heavy cream, egg, and vanilla.

In a separate large bowl, whisk together the flour, brown sugar, baking powder, and salt. Cut in the cold butter to the dry ingredients using a pastry blender, two knives, or your fingers (if you're fast, so the butter doesn't get too warm) until mixture resembles coarse crumbs. Add peanut butter chips and mix gently by hand.

Pour the wet mixture into the dry ingredients and stir until just combined and moistened. The dough will be wet. If you have a scone pan, lightly grease the pan and evenly distribute the dough into 8 scones. If you are using a baking sheet, either lightly grease, or line with parchment paper or a silicon baking mat. Using a 1/2 cup measuring cup or large spoon, drop the dough onto baking sheet, making eight equal size scones. Bake for 20-25 minutes or until slightly golden and set – a toothpick inserted in the middle should come out clean. Cool on a wire rack.

Once the scones are cooled, liberally drizzle the peanut butter glaze on top. While the glaze is still wet, sprinkle with the crispy, crumbled bacon as a finishing touch to make it truly Elvis style!

These are best if served the same day but can be refrigerated up to 2 or 3 days and reheated in the microwave or toaster oven. Enjoy!

Abby Kimball's Peanut Butter and Banana Scones
(photo courtesy of Abby Kimball)

Lamar and brother Troy

Lamar and Carla's poodle, Darby

Lamar and Carla—they don't normally dress this way

Lamar and Darby

www.ingramcontent.com/pod-product-compliance
Lightning Source LLC
Chambersburg PA
CBHW040813120626
46547CB00004B/528